Visual Geography Series®

ROMANIA

...in Pictures

Prepared by
Geography Department

Lerner Publications Company
Minneapolis

Photo by Bernice Condit

**A farmer transports a load of hay near Huedin, a village in
the Transylvania region of Romania.**

This book is an all-new edition in the Visual Geography Series. Previous editions were published by
Sterling Publishing Company, New York City. The
text, set in 10/12 Century Textbook, is fully revised
and updated, and new photogaphs, maps, charts, and
captions have been added.

LIBRARY OF CONGRESS CATALOGING-IN-PUBLICATION DATA

Romania in pictures / prepared by Geography
  Department, Lerner Publications Company.
    p. cm. – (Visual geography series)
  Includes index.
    Summary: Describes the topography, history, society,
  economy, and governmental structure of Romania.
    ISBN 0-8225-1894-5 (lib. bdg.)
    1. Romania–Juvenile literature. 2. Romania–
  Pictorial works–Juvenile literature. [1. Romania.] I.
  Lerner Publications Company. Geography Dept.
  II. Series: Visual geography series (Minneapolis, Minn.)
  DR206.R63 1993
  949.8–dc20   92-32861
                                           CIP
                                           AC

International Standard Book Number: 0-8225-1894-5
Library of Congress Catalog Card Number: 92-32861

VISUAL GEOGRAPHY SERIES®

Publisher
Harry Jonas Lerner
Senior Editor
Mary M. Rodgers
Editors
Gretchen Bratvold
Tom Streissguth
Colleen Sexton
Photo Researcher
Bill Kauffmann
Editorial/Photo Assistant
Marybeth Campbell
Consultants/Contributors
Paul Teodorescu
Sandra K. Davis
Designer
Jim Simondet
Cartographer
Carol F. Barrett
Indexer
Sylvia Timian
Production Manager
Gary J. Hansen

Photo by Bernice Condit

**In past centuries, many Romanians built their homes en-
tirely of wooden slats and shingles.**

Acknowledgments

Title page photo by Bryan Ney.

Elevation contours adapted from *The Times Atlas of
the World*, seventh comprehensive edition (New York:
Times Books, 1985).

Romanian accents, which affect Romanian
pronunciation, have not been used in this book.

Photo by Caroline Penn

Ethnic Germans in Transylvania celebrate with traditional German music and food. Throughout its history, this area has been settled by many different ethnic groups, including Germans, Hungarians, and Romanians.

Contents

UKRAINE

HUNGARY

MOLDOVA

Prut R.

MARAMURES

Suceava

B U K O V I N A

Moldova R.

• Voronet

Iasi

M O L D A V I A

Roman

UKRAINE

Somes R.

Huedin •

Cluj •

Tirgu-Mures •

T R A N S Y L V A N I A

Siret R.

Siria •

Copsa Mica •

B A N A T

Timisoara •

Mures R.

Sibiu •

Brasov •

Sinaia •

Focsani •

Galati •

Oh R.

Dimbovita R.

Tirgoviste •

DANUBE
DELTA

D O B R O G E A

Lake Razelm

Lake Sinoe

Histria (Ruins)

SERBIA

Draguseni •

Arges R.

Arges R.

W A L L A C H I A

BUCHAREST

Ialomita R.

Cernavoda •

Canal

Constanta

Danube

R.

BULGARIA

BLACK
SEA

ROMANIA

N

County and Municipal District
Boundaries

Major Roads

0   50   100 Miles

0   50   100 Kilometers

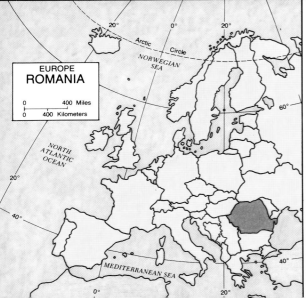

20°   0°   20°

Arctic   Circle

NORWEGIAN
SEA

EUROPE
ROMANIA

0   400 Miles

0   400 Kilometers

60°

NORTH
ATLANTIC
OCEAN

20°

40°

40°

MEDITERRANEAN SEA

0°

20°

METRIC CONVERSION CHART
To Find Approximate Equivalents

WHEN YOU KNOW:	MULTIPLY BY:	TO FIND:
AREA		
acres	0.41	hectares
square miles	2.59	square kilometers
CAPACITY		
gallons	3.79	liters
LENGTH		
feet	30.48	centimeters
yards	0.91	meters
miles	1.61	kilometers
MASS (weight)		
pounds	0.45	kilograms
tons	0.91	metric tons
VOLUME		
cubic yards	0.77	cubic meters
TEMPERATURE		
degrees Fahrenheit	0.56 (*after* subtracting 32)	degrees Celsius

Demonstrators gathered in Bucharest, the capital of Romania, during national elections in 1990. Although a rebellion had recently toppled Romania's Communist regime, these elections returned several former Communists to power.

Introduction

A nation of 23 million people in southeastern Europe, Romania is undergoing a difficult transformation. During a violent revolt in 1989, Romanians overthrew the dictatorship of Nicolae Ceausescu. A new constitution guaranteed civil rights and established an elected parliament. Nevertheless, Romanians are struggling to build a stable and democratic government. Serious economic problems are hurting the country, which has become one of the poorest in Europe.

Romanians trace their origins to the Dacians, who occupied the region as early as 1000 B.C. Rome, an empire founded on the Italian Peninsula, conquered ancient Dacia at the beginning of the second century A.D. Roman colonists raised cities, built new roads, and introduced the Latin language. After Rome withdrew from Dacia in the late third century, invaders from northern Europe and from Asia attacked eastern Europe. Further conflicts and invasions prevented Romanians from organizing independent states until the fourteenth century.

For much of their history, Romanians have lived in the shadow of stronger neighboring nations. In the fifteenth century, Hungarian landowners from central Europe and Turks from Asia Minor (modern Turkey) controlled large regions of Romania. The economy grew slowly and, at the beginning of the twentieth century, was still largely based on agriculture. Foreign political control also slowed Romania's unification. Modern Romania came into being after World War I ended in 1918.

During the next two decades, Romania experienced political turmoil and an economic depression. After World War II (1939–1945), the Soviet Union—Romania's neighbor to the east—supported a Communist takeover of Romania's government. The Communists brutally suppressed their opponents, executing some and jailing many others. The new regime also took over businesses and farms. Government planners managed the economy under the direction of Soviet leaders.

Young farm workers rest from harvesting potatoes in a Romanian field. Although many Romanians have left the countryside to work in the nation's large cities, others remained on state-owned "collective" farms, where much of the planting and harvesting had to be done by hand.

Houses, shops, and a church line a quiet street in Brasov, a city in the foothills of the Transylvanian Alps in central Romania.

After Ceausescu came to power in 1965, Romania formed ties with non-Communist nations in Europe. Although industrial production grew rapidly, the government borrowed heavily to pay for new housing and factories. Communist leaders also cut back on imports, which led to shortages of consumer goods, food, and energy. By the late 1980s, a declining standard of living was causing serious hardship for most Romanians.

After Ceausescu's downfall in December 1989, Romania's new president, Ion Iliescu, promised to improve the nation's economy. Having ended central planning, the government is selling state-owned businesses and attempting to put a free market in place. But former Communist officials still dominate Romanian politics, and many Romanian voters distrust their leaders. Despite its newly won democracy, Romania faces a difficult period of political reform and economic recovery.

Painters covered the outside walls of the fifteenth-century Voronet Monastery with portraits of Christian saints.

7

The Carpathian Mountains rise above the rolling hills of Moldavia, a region in northeastern Romania.

1) The Land

Romania is the largest nation in the Balkan Peninsula, a mountainous region that lies between the Adriatic Sea and the Black Sea in southeastern Europe. The country's neighbors include Hungary to the northwest, Serbia (part of the former Republic of Yugoslavia) to the southwest, and Bulgaria to the south. Moldova, an independent nation that was once a member of the Soviet Union, sits northeast of Romania. A border with Ukraine, another former Soviet republic, lies west and south of Moldova. Romania also has 130 miles of coastline along the Black Sea in the southeast.

With a land area of 91,699 square miles, Romania is slightly smaller than the state of Oregon. The greatest distance from north to south is 320 miles. From west to east, Romania stretches 460 miles.

Topography

Romania's landscape includes mountains, forests, rolling plains, and swampy lowlands. The Carpathian Mountains curve through the center of the country, dividing the country's three largest regions— Transylvania in the northwest, Moldavia in the northeast, and Wallachia in the south. Most settlement has taken place on the plains and in the mountain foothills.

THE CARPATHIANS AND TRANSYLVANIA

The Carpathian Mountains extend from the border with Ukraine southward and

8

then westward through the middle of Romania. Several peaks in the Carpathians reach 8,000 feet in elevation. Wide river valleys provide routes for road and rail traffic through the mountains. Glaciers (slow-moving masses of ice) carved small freshwater lakes within the Carpathians during the most recent Ice Age, which ended about 10,000 years ago.

The Romanian Carpathians are made up of three smaller ranges—the Moldavian Carpathians in the north, the Transylvanian Alps in the south and southwest, and the Western Carpathians in the west. The Transylvanian Alps have the highest average elevation—5,000 feet—as well as the country's tallest peak, 8,343-foot Mount Moldoveanul.

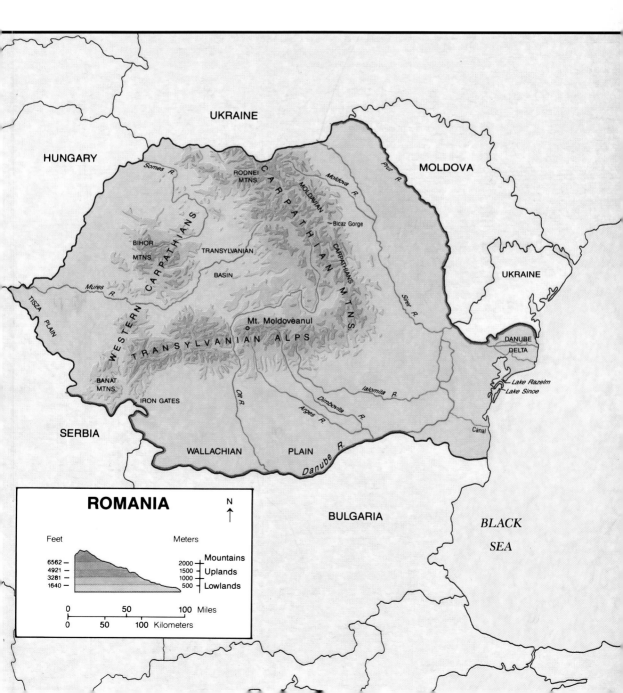

The Transylvanian Basin, an area of hills and river valleys, extends across northwestern Romania. Smaller mountain ranges exist in Transylvania, where the average elevation is 1,200 feet. The Bihor Mountains rise west of the city of Cluj. The Rodnei Mountains, a spur of the Carpathians, lie near Romania's northern border with Ukraine.

Bukovina, northeast of Transylvania, is a thickly forested area in the foothills of the Carpathians. The Banat region lies between Transylvania and Romania's border with Serbia. The fertile plains of Banat continue into Serbia and Hungary.

PLAINS AND LOWLANDS

Rolling plains dominate the landscape of eastern and southern Romania. Moldavia lies between the Carpathian Mountains and the Prut River. Wallachia stretches from the Transylvanian Alps southward to the Danube River.

The Dobrogea region in southeastern Romania has the country's lowest average elevation. Some areas of Dobrogea near the Black Sea are only a few feet above sea level. Swamps and reed marshes are common along the Danube, which flows northward through Dobrogea before emptying into the Black Sea.

Rivers

The Danube River, Europe's second longest waterway, forms part of Romania's borders with Serbia and Bulgaria. The busy river, which carries passenger boats and commercial barges, crosses the Carpathian Mountains within a narrow pass known since ancient times as the Iron Gates. After flowing through southern Romania, the Danube curves northward in Dobrogea, where a canal carries river traffic to the Black Sea just south of the port of Constanta.

Photo by Caroline Penn

Pollution from factories in the village of Copsa Mica, in Transylvania, has left a thin film of soot over the streets.

At the Village Museum in Bucharest, traditional rural homes and industries —including a small mill—are on display.

In the 1970s, a new dam raised the Danube's level and eased navigation through the Iron Gates. The river has become an important source of hydroelectric power and of irrigation water for farming. But the Danube has also suffered heavy pollution from industries and from wastes poured into it by the cities along its banks.

Romania's other major waterways are tributaries of the Danube. The Mures River runs westward between the Transylvanian Alps and the Bihor Mountains. After flowing through the lowlands of Banat, the Mures crosses Romania's border with Hungary and joins the Tisza River, another Danube tributary.

Many rivers flow southward from the Transylvanian Alps through Wallachia to the Danube. The Olt River forms a wide valley in the mountains before reaching the Wallachian Plain. The Arges and the Ialomita rivers cross eastern Wallachia near Bucharest, Romania's capital.

The Moldova and Siret rivers, which rise in the Carpathian Mountains, are the major waterways in Moldavia. The Prut River, which forms Romania's border with

Children play in a small river during the late summer, Romania's dry season. Families from a nearby village also use the stream for washing their clothes and to draw water for cooking.

A floral pedestal blooms in Bucharest's Herastrau Park, where lakes and spacious lawns attract residents and tourists.

Moldova, meets the Danube River just west of the Danube delta.

Climate

Romania has a variable climate with warm summers and cold winters. Mild winds from the west and south moderate colder air that blows from the plains of Ukraine. Summer temperatures are generally lower in Romania's mountainous regions and higher in the plains of Moldavia and Wallachia.

In Transylvania, higher average elevations contribute to a cooler climate. In addition, winds that blow from the Adriatic Sea to the west lower Transylvania's summer temperatures. The lowlands and plains of eastern and southern Romania experience greater temperature extremes. Bucharest averages 73° F in July, the warmest month, and 27° F in January, the coldest month.

Precipitation is heaviest in Transylvania and in the Carpathian Mountains, where

Rowboats line a wooden dock at Lacul Rosu (Red Lake), a natural lake in the highlands of Transylvania.

An Orthodox cathedral towers over the center of Timisoara, the largest city of the Banat region in western Romania.

an average of 53 inches of rain and snow fall each year. Throughout the country, most rainfall occurs in spring and autumn. Dobrogea is Romania's warmest and driest region, with less than 15 inches of annual rainfall.

Flora and Fauna

Thick forests once grew on the plains and mountains of Romania. Although Romanians have cleared much of the land for settlement and for agriculture, forests still cover more than 25 percent of the country. Coniferous (evergreen) trees, such as pine and spruce, flourish in the Carpathian Mountains and in the higher elevations of Transylvania. Above the timberline—where temperatures are too low to support trees—hardy lichens and mosses take root in thin soil and on the surfaces of bare rocks.

Flowers and shrubbery decorate the open courtyard of Romania's Agapia Monastery.

Large, mixed forests of coniferous and deciduous (leaf-shedding) trees thrive in Transylvania. Deciduous trees, including birch, beech, and oak, favor the warmer climate of the plains. Willows and poplars line the banks of the Danube and other rivers, and reeds flourish in the swampy Danube delta.

In places where Romanian cities and farms have not eliminated natural habitats, a variety of wildlife survives. Wild boars, foxes, and chamois—small, goatlike antelopes—live in the Carpathians. Deer, wolves, and lynxes also inhabit these mountains, as well as sparsely populated regions of Transylvania.

The Danube Delta supports many varieties of birds and other wildlife. In spring and autumn, birds migrating between Europe and Africa pass over the region. Nightingales, egrets, spoonbills, cormo-rants, geese, eagles, and ospreys nest in the marshes. Large flocks of pelicans inhabit the northern delta.

Trout flourish in Romania's mountain lakes. Pike, carp, flounder, and salmon live in the rivers and along the Black Sea coast. Eggs from Black Sea sturgeon provide caviar, an important Romanian export.

Natural Resources

Romania's most valuable resources are natural gas and oil. Deposits of these fuels exist in the foothills of the Carpathian Mountains, near the Danube valley, and in Moldavia. Dobrogea and Moldavia also have natural gas as well as coal. Uranium, the fuel used in nuclear power plants, has been mined in Transylvania and Moldavia. Over time, most of Romania's energy resources have been exhausted, and

The dam at the Bicaz Gorge provides electricity for cities in Moldavia. Water power is generating an increasing percentage of the country's energy.

14

Photo by Patricia Drentea/Visuals Unlimited

Romania's Communist government destroyed an entire neighborhood to construct the Street of Socialist Victory, a wide boulevard in downtown Bucharest. In the background is a gigantic palace built under orders from Nicolae Ceausescu, Romania's president until 1989.

the country must import much of the natural gas, coal, and oil it needs to generate heat and electricity.

Romania's minerals include copper, zinc, and bauxite (the raw material used to manufacture aluminum). Gold and silver mines have been worked since ancient times in the northern Carpathians. Lead and salt deposits exist in Transylvania.

The current of the Danube River powers large hydroelectric plants. Reeds growing in the river's delta provide a fiber used to manufacture paper. Extensive forests in Transylvania and in the Carpathians supply lumber for Romania's building industry and for export.

Cities

Bucharest, a city of two million people, lies on the Dimbovita River in eastern Wallachia. A commercial and transportation hub, Bucharest is also Romania's largest manufacturing center. Factories in the city

Independent Picture Service

The imposing Arch of Triumph stands in the center of Bucharest. The arch was built during the 1930s in the style of the famous Arc de Triomphe, a monument in the French capital of Paris.

15

Small groups of people gather on a rainy day in Bucharest. Many of the capital's buildings date to the nineteenth century.

produce machinery, plastics, rubber, clothing, and electronic equipment.

Bucharest grew as a settlement along a major Balkan trading route. By the fourteenth century, the city had become the headquarters of the princes of Wallachia. In 1862, after Moldavia and Wallachia united to form Romania, Bucharest became the new nation's capital. Foreign armies occupied the city during both World War I (1914–1918) and World War II. Later, the Romanian Communist government destroyed traditional buildings and entire neighborhoods to make way for

An opera house sits at the end of a long, green boulevard in Timisoara. A cultural center dating to the thirteenth century, Timisoara also boasts theaters, libraries, a university, and an imposing castle.

An old Turkish mosque (Islamic house of prayer) still stands in Constanta, Romania's largest Black Sea port. Founded on the site of the ancient Greek city of Tomis, Constanta was under the control of the Ottoman (Turkish) Empire for several centuries. The town has extensive archaeological remains, as well as wide beaches, to attract visitors.

modern office buildings and a new presidential palace.

Brasov (population 351,000), the nation's second largest city, lies on a high plateau in the foothills of the Transylvanian Alps. Founded by the Teutonic Knights, a German military brotherhood, Brasov dates to A.D. 1211. Although it has become an important industrial city with car and chemical factories, Brasov has preserved a central core of ancient homes and churches. Bran Castle, an imposing fortress that once guarded Transylvania's frontier with Wallachia, is a popular tourist attraction that lies 20 miles from Brasov.

Greek traders founded Constanta (population 328,000), a port on Romania's Black Sea coast, in the sixth century B.C. A canal links the port to the Danube River. From Constanta, Romanian companies export a wide variety of industrial goods. Tourists travel to Constanta to enjoy nearby resorts along the Black Sea and to visit the extensive ruins of ancient Greek and Roman buildings.

Cluj (population 310,000) lies on the Somes River in central Transylvania. German settlers changed the original Latin name of the settlement—Napoca—in the twelfth century. The city now appears on many maps as Cluj-Napoca. For much of its history Cluj was controlled by Hungarians, who owned many estates in Transylvania until the early twentieth century. The city still contains a large Hungarian population. Factories in Cluj produce chemicals, textiles, and ceramics.

The largest city of the Banat region is Timisoara (population 325,000), a commercial and industrial hub near the Serbian border. Factories in Timisoara make

Pedestrians stroll through Timisoara, a city that has preserved much of its traditional architecture.

chemicals, shoes, and electrical equipment. Timisoara has also become a cultural center, with theaters, libraries, and a major university.

Iasi (population 313,000), in northeastern Romania, is the historic capital of Moldavia. Located near Romania's border with Moldova, Iasi has been conquered and occupied several times in its history. In the early 1800s, the city was a headquarters for the movement to unite the regions that make up modern Romania. Industries in Iasi include furniture and pharmaceutical factories, ironworks, and textile mills. Iasi also has many scientific and cultural institutes.

Iasi, the largest city in Moldavia, was the temporary capital of Romania during World War I. The city is home to a wide variety of industries as well as an important university.

A doorway remains standing in the ruins of Histria, an ancient Greek city on the Black Sea coast. Histria and other ports in the area traded with cities in Asia Minor (modern Turkey) and eastern Europe.

Photo by Paul E. Michelson

2) History and Government

Humans have been living in the area of modern Romania for at least 12,000 years. The first group to build large settlements in the region, the Thracians, migrated from the north and west to the Carpathian Mountains and into the Danube River Valley. The Thracians were skilled farmers who raised grains, grapevines, and herds of cattle on their lands.

A Thracian group known as the Dacians developed an independent state north of the Danube River in about 1000 B.C. The Dacians prospered from trade with Greek merchants who had established ports along the western coast of the Black Sea. Ancient Dacians also controlled trade along the Danube River. The region's deposits of copper and iron ore enabled the Dacians to make strong weapons, and Dacia gradually became one of the most advanced and powerful realms in southeastern Europe.

Roman Settlement

Dacia's fertile soil, as well as its gold and silver deposits, attracted foreign invaders. By the second century B.C., Rome, a growing state based on the Italian Peninsula, was conquering large areas of the Balkan Peninsula. At first, the Romans and Dacians cooperated to build trading

19

posts and fortifications in the Danube valley. Later, the Dacians fought for control of the region's resources. The Dacian king Burebista led violent raids on Roman settlements until his death in 44 B.C.

For two centuries, the Dacians successfully defended their territory from Roman attacks across the Danube. But the Roman emperor Trajan, who took power in A.D. 98, was determined to conquer Dacia and to seize its valuable mines. Trajan's army finally defeated the Dacians in A.D. 106.

Trajan posted a large Roman force in Dacia and colonized the region with farmers, traders, and soldiers from other parts of the Roman Empire. The Romans built cities, roads, forts, and farming estates. The new colonists spoke Latin, the language of the Romans, and the Dacians eventually adopted this tongue. Modern Romania traces its name as well as its language to this period of Roman occupation.

Migrations in Eastern Europe

Despite Rome's military strength, Goths and Sarmatians from the north and east besieged Dacian towns in the third century A.D. Few of these invaders settled within Dacia's borders, but the repeated attacks forced the Roman army to withdraw in A.D. 271. The Roman colonists and Dacian peasants remained behind, becoming the ancestors of the modern Romanians.

From the third through the fifth centuries, Romania remained a violent and chaotic territory, with no organized government and weak defenses. Visigoths, Huns, Bulgars, and Avars came from the north and east, destroying homes and farms. Eastern European Slavs also passed through the region on their way to settle lands south and west of the Danube. Dacian and Roman inhabitants fled into the Carpathian Mountains and into Transylvania.

The Roman emperor Trajan (left) conquered the province of Dacia in A.D. 106. To celebrate the defeat of the Dacians, which he considered one of his greatest achievements, Trajan ordered the building of a magnificent victory column that still stands in the city of Rome.

This Orthodox church and bell tower are in the town of Draguseni. Romanians have followed the Eastern Orthodox religion since the eleventh century, when Christianity split into Roman Catholic and Orthodox branches.

Photo by Bernice Condit

At the same time, the weakening Roman Empire was splitting into western and eastern halves. In the fifth century, the Western Empire collapsed after a series of invasions. The Eastern Roman (or Byzantine) Empire, with its capital at Constantinople (modern Istanbul), survived. The Byzantine Empire controlled lands south of the Danube River on the Balkan Peninsula.

From this region, Byzantine culture and religion spread northward through the Balkan Peninsula. Many Dacians and Romans practiced the Christian faith, which the Byzantine emperors had adopted. Missionaries from the Byzantine Empire also converted the Slavs in Europe to Christianity. Later, when the Christian church divided into Roman Catholic and Eastern Orthodox branches, Romania became an Orthodox stronghold.

Magyars and Tatars Invade

In the late ninth century, central Asian Magyars—the ancestors of the modern Hungarians—moved into southeastern Europe, conquering lands along the Danube. The Magyars settled new cities and converted to the Roman Catholic faith. In search of fertile cropland, they later pushed southward into Transylvania.

The Tatar chief Batu Khan led a huge force into eastern Europe in the thirteenth century, destroying villages and farms. The Tatar army soon retreated, but their invasion left much of Romania in ruins.

In the year 1000, the Roman Catholic pope crowned the Magyar leader Stephen I as king of Hungary, a land that included Transylvania. Although Stephen's successors tried to convert the people of Transylvania to Catholicism, most of the Romanians living in the region refused to abandon Orthodox Christianity.

To strengthen their control over Transylvania, the Hungarian kings offered land to German Catholics from northern Europe. These landowners adopted a feudal system that forced Romanian farmers to pay a portion of their harvests to the newcomers. Although Romanians still made up

In the fifteenth century, the *voivode* (ruler) of Moldavia built this fortress in Suceava, the Moldavian capital, to protect the region from eastern raiders.

The princes of Wallachia made their home at this palace at Tirgoviste. In times of conflict, the princes and their courts could retreat to the palace's defensive tower.

a majority of Transylvania's inhabitants, many became poor peasants or serfs— landless farm workers—on Transylvanian estates.

In 1241 Tatars from Asia swept across Moldavia and Transylvania and crushed the Hungarian armies. Although the Tatars retreated in the next year, the Hungarian king began to lose his hold on Transylvania. In the late thirteenth century, Transylvanian nobles formed their own diet, or legislature. At the same time, these landowners were demanding higher crop payments and seizing land owned by the peasants.

New Principalities

To escape these harsh conditions, many Romanians fled Transylvania to settle lands east and south of the Carpathian Mountains. Some of these refugees established their own small states, known as *voivodates,* in Wallachia and Moldavia.

Boyars—landowning nobles—in the voivodates raised money by renting their land to peasants. Many boyars also became important government officials or advisers to the *voivodes*—the rulers of the voivodates.

Although Hungary attempted to extend its control to these regions, the Romanians fought to keep their independence. Prince Basarab defeated Hungarian forces in 1330 and established the principality (prince's realm) of Wallachia. In 1349 a Transylvanian leader named Bogdan crossed the Carpathians to found a new state along the Moldova River in northeastern Romania. Ten years later, Bogdan's lands became the independent principality of Moldavia, which extended from the Carpathian Mountains to the Dniester River in what is now Moldova.

Councils made up of boyars and Orthodox clergy elected the princes of Moldavia and Wallachia. The princes had the power to

A European prince falls to his knees before the sultan (ruler) of the Ottoman Empire. The sultan ruled the conquered territories of eastern Europe through local kings and princes, who collected taxes and provided troops for the Turkish army.

Courtesy of Cultural and Tourism Office of the Turkish Embassy

grant land and noble titles to the boyars. But frequent struggles broke out among those claiming the title of prince. These rivalries weakened the principalities, leaving them vulnerable to invasion.

Attack of the Ottoman Turks

In the fourteenth century, the Ottoman Turks of Asia Minor attacked the Balkan Peninsula. The Turks conquered lands south of the Danube and in 1391 crossed the river into Wallachia. Mircea the Old, the prince of Wallachia, allied with the king of Hun-

gary to fight the Turks. But Ottoman forces defeated the Hungarian army in 1396, and in 1417 Mircea signed a peace treaty with the Turks. Under the agreement, Wallachia remained independent but was forced to pay a tribute of money and goods every year to the Ottoman sultan (ruler).

The Turks, who followed the Islamic religion, allowed Romanian princes to rule their territories and Orthodox Christians to practice their faith. But the forced tributes caused hardship in Moldavia and Wallachia. In 1453 the Turks overthrew the Byzantine Empire after capturing Constantinople.

Because the Romanians had traded through this city, its conquest by the Turks caused further economic decline in the principalities.

STEPHEN THE GREAT

Resistance to the Turks continued after the Ottoman conquest of Constantinople. In the late fifteenth century, the Moldavian prince Stephen the Great fortified his capital of Suceava and organized a force of peasants to fight the sultan. Stephen, who had successfully battled the Turks in Wallachia in the 1470s, tried to convince other European nations to join him in a crusade against the Islamic Turks.

Devoutly religious and a patron of the arts, Stephen hired skilled architects to build new Orthodox churches and monasteries throughout Moldavia. He also expanded the principality's trade with Europe and with the Middle East. Although the economy of Moldavia improved, Stephen was unable to convince the Christian rulers of Europe to assist him in his crusade.

Independent Picture Service

The Wallachian prince Vlad Tepes (Vlad the Impaler) gained a reputation for violence during his reign in the fifteenth century. Vlad's cruelty was the source of frightening folk legends in Romania. Centuries after his death in 1477 he became the model for Dracula, a character described in books, plays, and films.

Photo by Patricia Drentea/Visuals Unlimited

The grave of Stephen the Great, Moldavia's most famous ruler, lies within the Putna Monastery.

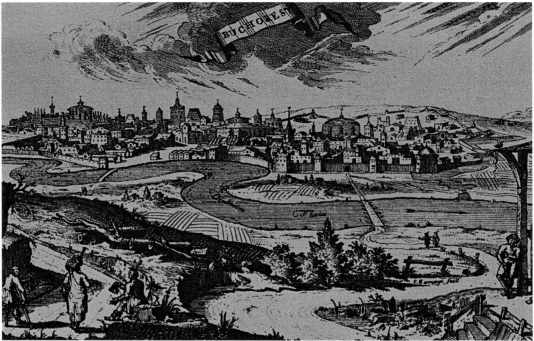

An early print shows Bucharest and the banks of the Dimbovita River. Bucharest became the capital of Wallachia in the seventeenth century.

The builder of this house, which dates to the 1600s, used thick walls and narrow windows to defend against attacks by the Turks and by other hostile forces.

After his death in 1504, the Moldavian princes became vassals (deputies) of the Turkish sultan.

REBELLION AND REFORMATION

Aided by unrest in the region, the armies of the sultan were still marching northward through the Balkan Peninsula. In Transylvania, a violent peasant revolt against Hungarian landowners broke out in 1514. Although the rebellion failed, the conflict weakened the Hungarian army. The Turks scored a decisive victory at Mohács in Hungary in 1526. Buda, the Hungarian capital, fell in 1541. Transylvania became a semi-independent region where the Turks collected taxes and stationed troops to guard against attack by western European armies. Although the Hungarian kings were overthrown, Hungarian nobles in Transylvania were allowed to appoint a prince and to form a parliament.

Later in the sixteenth century, a movement to reform the Roman Catholic Church arose in northern Europe. Protestants—followers of this movement—arrived in Transylvania and converted many of the region's northern European and Hungarian inhabitants to their faith. In the 1570s, the Transylvanian parliament granted freedom of worship to both Catholics and Protestants. This action did not improve the lives of the Orthodox Romanians, who continued to suffer harsh conditions in the service of Transylvanian nobles.

MICHAEL THE BRAVE

By this time, Moldavia and Wallachia were losing all traces of their independence. The Ottoman sultan demanded larger tributes and appointed foreign princes as rulers. Most of the Romanian inhabitants remained poor laborers on the estates of the boyars.

A few energetic and skillful leaders improved conditions in the seventeenth century. One of these was the Wallachian prince Michael the Brave, who gained his position by bribing the sultan. Michael led

Michael the Brave won brilliant victories against the Turks and united Transylvania, Moldavia, and Wallachia in the early 1600s.

his forces into Transylvania in 1599. To strengthen his control of the region, Michael allied with the area's Hungarian nobles. In 1600 he conquered Moldavia, bringing Wallachia, Moldavia, and Transylvania under a single Romanian leader for the first time.

Habsburg and Ottoman Rivalry

Michael's successes stirred his rivals to action. The ruler of the Habsburg Empire—a huge central European realm that controlled parts of Hungary—urged the Transylvanian nobles to resist Michael. The kingdom of Poland, which lay to the north of the Carpathian Mountains, attacked Moldavia. In 1601 a Habsburg general arranged to have the Romanian leader assassinated.

After Michael's death, the principalities again came under Turkish control. Most princes ruled for only a short time, and the fierce rivalry among them resulted in political turmoil. In addition, Moldavia and Wallachia were growing poorer. To maintain their wealth, the boyars seized peasant lands, and princes levied heavy taxes to bribe the sultan for their titles.

Matthew Basarab became prince of Wallachia in 1632. A skillful leader, Basarab ruled for 22 years and promoted cultural life within his state. Religious books were published, and Basarab's administrators drew up new law codes. In 1659 the Wallachians moved their capital from Tirgoviste, in the foothills of the Carpathians, to Bucharest, in the plains to the south. From this city, the Wallachian princes could more easily control trade in the region.

Farther north, the Turks were losing ground. Habsburg armies defeated a Turkish siege of Vienna, the capital of the Habsburg Empire, in 1683. At the same time, Transylvania's Hungarian princes were improving agriculture and building up their military forces. In 1688 the Turks retreated from Transylvania, and by 1700 the region was brought into the Habsburg

Courtesy of Embassy of Romania

Prince Constantin Brancoveanu of Wallachia was a popular leader who planned extensive building projects in his state. But after asking for help from Russia to resist the forces of the Ottoman Empire, Brancoveanu was captured and executed by the Turks in 1714.

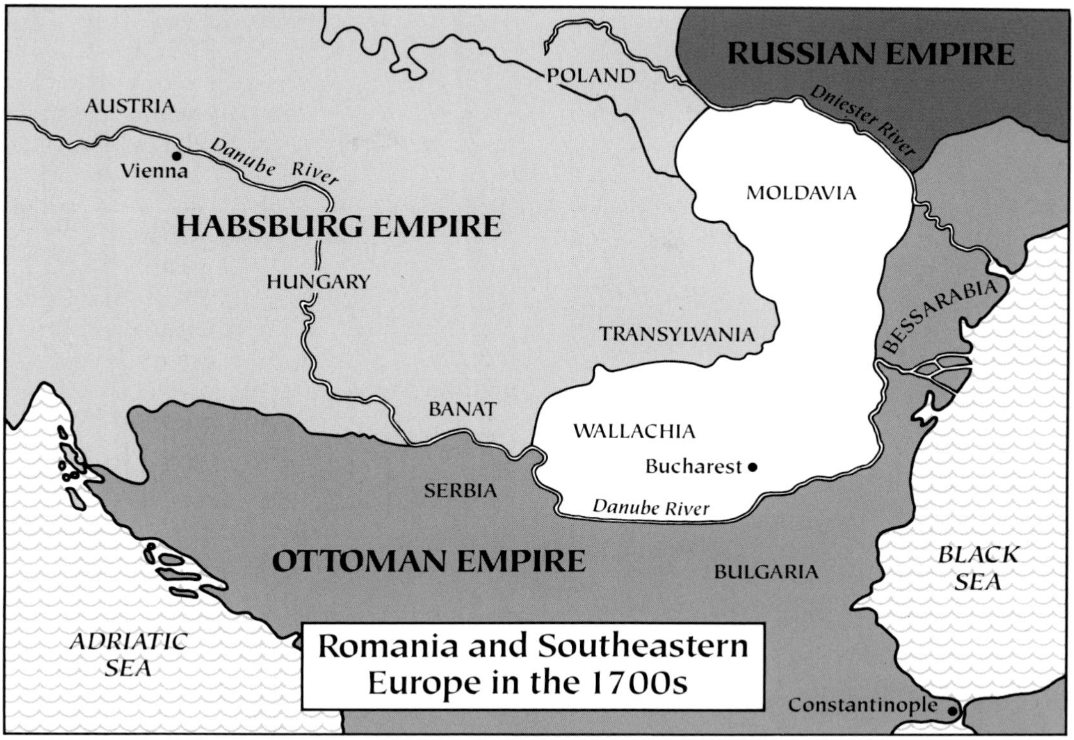
RUSSIAN EMPIRE
POLAND
AUSTRIA
Dniester River
Vienna
Danube River
MOLDAVIA
HABSBURG EMPIRE
HUNGARY
BESSARABIA
TRANSYLVANIA
BANAT
WALLACHIA
Bucharest
SERBIA
Danube River
OTTOMAN EMPIRE
BULGARIA
BLACK SEA
ADRIATIC SEA
Romania and Southeastern Europe in the 1700s
Constantinople

Artwork by Laura Westlund

In the eighteenth century, as Ottoman strength declined, Romania and the rest of southeastern Europe became the scene of conflict among several neighboring powers. To gain greater independence from the Turks, Romanian leaders allied with the Habsburg and Russian empires.

—or Austrian—Empire. This did not improve conditions for the area's Romanians, most of whom remained poor serfs with few legal rights.

The Phanariot Princes

As Turkish strength declined, neighboring states tried to gain control of the Romanian principalities. Dimitri Cantemir—a Moldavian leader and a famous historian—allied with Russia, an empire to the east whose people also practiced the Orthodox faith. In 1711 Cantemir led a revolt against the Turks, winning the support of the Russian czar (emperor) and the prince of Wallachia. Although this uprising failed, Cantemir's books and ideas awakened nationalism among Romanian-speaking people in the region.

After Cantemir's revolt, the Ottoman Empire regained control over the principalities. The sultan appointed loyal officials from the Phanar neighborhood of Istanbul to rule Wallachia and Moldavia. In this way, the Turks hoped to stop any future rebellion among the Romanians.

Most of the Phanariot princes used the principalities solely to enrich themselves. The Phanariots heavily taxed the boyars and peasants in both Moldavia and Wallachia, causing the economies of these two states to decline. Many boyars lost their properties, and many peasants were reduced to serfdom.

In 1791 these harsh conditions prompted the Wallachian boyars to ask the Russians for help in ending the rule of the Phanariots. This led to many years of conflict between Russia and Turkey over Romanian

The military commander Tudor Vladimirescu became a national hero after leading a revolt against the Phanariot princes—foreigners whom the Turks were appointing to govern Moldavia and Wallachia.

territory. In 1812 the Peace of Bucharest formally recognized Turkish control of Wallachia and Moldavia. Russia seized Bessarabia, the part of Moldavia that lay east of the Prut River.

A New Constitution

Unable to control the vast territory it had conquered, the Ottoman Empire began weakening in the nineteenth century. Tudor Vladimirescu, a Wallachian officer, saw this as an opportunity to overthrow Phanariot rule. In 1821 he led an uprising against the Phanariot leaders. Although

Vladimirescu directs a crossing of the Olt River during the revolt of 1821. Although Vladimirescu was captured and executed, his rebellion forced the Ottoman sultan to name Romanian princes to rule the principalities.

Vladimirescu was murdered, the Ottoman Empire agreed to begin appointing Romanian princes.

Seeking to gain control of the Balkan region, Russia invaded Moldavia and Wallachia in 1828, touching off another Russo-Turkish conflict. The Treaty of Adrianople, signed by Russia and Turkey in 1829, allowed Russian armies to occupy Moldavia and Wallachia. Although the principalities still belonged to the Ottoman Empire, Romanian princes were permitted to rule Moldavia and Wallachia for life.

In the 1830s, with Russian forces still present in the region, Romanians drew up their first constitution. Known as the Organic Statutes, this document called for an assembly of landowners and the unification of Moldavia and Wallachia. New laws also reformed the taxation and court systems, established public schools, and provided for the assembly to appoint future Romanian princes. But the Organic Statutes also permitted the Russians to station troops in the principalities. For this reason, many Romanians later denounced the document.

In Transylvania, Hungarians were pressing for the unification of the region with Hungary, which was still a part of the Habsburg Empire. Their opportunity came in 1848, as popular revolutions spread throughout Europe. Like many other Europeans, Hungarians were demanding elected governments and an end to the privileges of monarchs and nobles. In response to these demands, the Transylvanian legislature abolished serfdom and curbed the rights enjoyed by Transylvania's landowners.

The legislature also voted to join Transylvania with Hungary, a decision that touched off a violent conflict in Transylvania between Hungarians and Romanians. The forces of the Austrian emperor —who was opposed to further Hungarian expansion—fought alongside the Romanians. After the Russian czar sent military forces into the region to help the Austrians, the fighting ended. Austria then took direct control of Transylvania.

Although the Romanian farmers in Transylvania were freed from serfdom, they were still living in poverty on unproductive land. To escape these conditions, many Romanians crossed the Carpathian Mountains to Moldavia and Wallachia.

Unification

The revolutions of 1848 had inspired many Romanians to fight for a unified Romanian nation. New political parties arose to press for complete independence from Russia and Turkey. In May a revolt in Wallachia led to the establishment of a new Romanian constitution. But after Russian and Turkish armies invaded Bucharest, the rebels fled the capital and the new constitution was abolished by force.

Nicolae Balcescu helped spark the uprising of 1848 in Wallachia. A coalition of Russian and Turkish forces defeated the rebellion, after which the Wallachian governor banished Balcescu to Sicily, an island in the Mediterranean Sea.

Prince Carol, a member of a German royal family, was elected prince of Romania by a popular vote in 1866. In 1881, when Romania became a kingdom, Prince Carol took the title of King Carol I.

After Russia lost a war against Turkey in 1856, a conference of several European powers guaranteed the political rights of Romanians in the principalities. Three years later, assemblies in Moldavia and Wallachia elected Colonel Alexandru Ioan Cuza as their prince. In 1861 the two principalities united to form Romania. The country's first national legislature began meeting in Bucharest.

Cuza passed important land reforms, ended serfdom in Moldavia and Wallachia, and allowed freed serfs to own land. But corruption weakened his administration, and many Romanian legislators and landowners opposed the new laws. In 1866 army officers broke into Cuza's palace in Bucharest and forced him to resign his office. Succeeding Cuza was Prince Carol, a member of a European royal family who became the Romanian ruler through a plebiscite (popular vote).

Political conditions were also changing rapidly in Transylvania. In 1867 Austria was fighting wars on several fronts in central Europe. To compromise with the Hungarians, the Habsburg emperor Franz Joseph agreed to the creation of a dual (two-part) monarchy known as Austria-Hungary. At the same time, Hungary directly annexed (took over) Transylvania.

Independence

In 1877 Russia and Turkey again went to war. The Romanians provided an army to help the Russians, who quickly gained the upper hand in the fighting. Under the terms of the Treaty of Berlin, which ended the conflict in the next year, Russia and Turkey officially recognized Romanian independence. The treaty also granted the northern part of the Dobrogea region to Romania. (Bulgaria held southern Dobrogea.)

In 1881 Romania's parliament proclaimed the nation to be a kingdom, and Prince Carol became King Carol I. With few allies in the Balkan region, Carol sought to strengthen his nation's ties with western Europe. Romanian artists, writers, and politicians traveled to France to study, work, and exchange ideas. In addition, Carol's nephew and heir married the niece of Queen Victoria, the British monarch.

During Carol's reign, new industries grew in several Romanian cities. Oil reserves discovered in Wallachia became a valuable source of export income. The busy port of Constanta improved the

nation's foreign trade. The government planned new roads and built rural schools. Despite these advances, many Romanian peasants and workers still suffered poor living conditions.

Balkan Conflicts

Although many Balkan countries had gained their independence from the Ottoman Empire, conflict was common in the region at the beginning of the twentieth

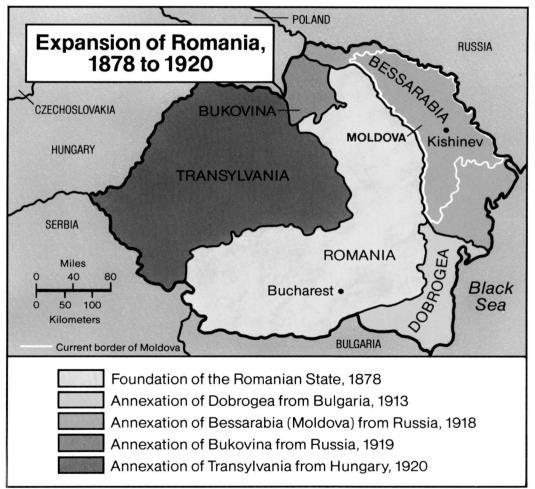

Expansion of Romania, 1878 to 1920

POLAND

RUSSIA

CZECHOSLOVAKIA

BESSARABIA

BUKOVINA

HUNGARY

MOLDOVA · Kishinev

TRANSYLVANIA

SERBIA

Miles
0   40   80

0   50   100
Kilometers

ROMANIA

Bucharest ·

DOBROGEA

Black Sea

—— Current border of Moldova

BULGARIA

☐ Foundation of the Romanian State, 1878
☐ Annexation of Dobrogea from Bulgaria, 1913
☐ Annexation of Bessarabia (Moldova) from Russia, 1918
☐ Annexation of Bukovina from Russia, 1919
☐ Annexation of Transylvania from Hungary, 1920

Artwork by Laura Westlund

As the result of wars in eastern Europe, the kingdom of Romania added several regions to its territory. After the Balkan War of 1913, Bulgaria lost control of Dobrogea. Bessarabia (modern Moldova) and Bukovina became Romanian territory after World War I (1914–1918). Hungary lost Transylvania to Romania as part of a treaty signed in 1920.

A Romanian artillery unit prepares for action during World War I.

Romanian soldiers march into Transylvania, an area settled for centuries by Romanians and Hungarians. After World War I, Hungary signed an agreement yielding the region to Romania.

century. Bulgaria and several of its allies fought Turkey in 1912 and quickly defeated the Ottoman forces. At first, Romania stayed neutral. But after Bulgaria turned against its allies in 1913, Romania invaded Bulgaria and southern Dobrogea. After suffering a rapid defeat, Bulgaria gave up southern Dobrogea to Romania.

In the summer of 1914, the Balkan conflicts flared into an international war, with the Central Powers of Austria-Hungary and Germany pitted against Russia, Britain, and France (the Allies). At the outbreak of World War I, many Romanians were demanding that Austria-Hungary surrender Transylvania to Romania. But the king and the Romanian parliament, hoping to stay out of the war, declared that Romania would remain neutral.

When Carol died in 1914, his nephew Ferdinand inherited the throne. In 1916 Romania—with promises of support from the Allies—sent forces into Transylvania to claim the region. But a combined force of Austrians, Germans, and Bulgarians crushed the Romanian army. German forces marched into Bucharest, and the Romanian government fled the capital. Romania then withdrew from the war.

In 1918, as the Central Powers were suffering defeat, Romania again fought for Transylvania. For a brief period, the Romanian army was able to occupy Budapest, Hungary's capital. After the war ended in November 1918, Romania gained Transylvania and part of the Banat region. Bessarabia declared its independence from Russia and joined Romania.

Between the Wars

The Romanian legislature enacted sweeping changes in the years immediately following the war. The legislature adopted a new constitution in 1923 and attempted to meet unrest in the countryside with a program of land reforms. The government also restructured and modernized Romania's industries.

In 1921 a group of Romanian politicians formed the Romanian Communist party. The Communists sought to put all property and industry under government control. A Communist government had already taken power in Russia and later formed the Soviet Union. Nevertheless, for many years the Romanian Communist party remained very small.

Romania's most powerful political party during the 1920s—the Liberal party—was headed by Ion Bratianu, who became prime minister in the mid-1920s. Several other smaller parties shared power with the Liberals. The National Peasant party, led by Iuliu Maniu, opposed the Liberal party and gained the support of many rural workers. Maniu became prime minister after the National Peasant party won elections in 1928.

Romania's economy declined in the 1930s, when a global depression was causing severe unemployment in Europe. Rivalry between the Liberal and National Peasant parties weakened the government, making it possible for more extreme political groups to gain influence.

A merchant delivers kerosene by horse-drawn carriage in Bucharest. Romanians suffered shortages of food and fuel in the years following World War I.

In the 1930s, a movement known as the Iron Guard won support among Romanians who were unhappy with the country's divided parliament. The Iron Guard staged violent antigovernment demonstrations in Bucharest, and in 1933 Iron Guard members assassinated the Romanian prime minister. Corneliu Codreanu, the leader of the Iron Guard, supported the German dictator Adolf Hitler, who had come to power as head of the Nazi party in 1933.

Seeking to stop the growing unrest, King Carol II—who had inherited the throne in 1930—suspended the Romanian legislature and abolished the constitution. After assuming dictatorial powers, Carol ordered the arrest and execution of Codreanu and other leaders of the Iron Guard. Carol also signed an economic pact with Hitler that allowed Germany to develop Romania's natural resources.

In the late 1930s, Hitler's armies invaded several nations in central Europe. These actions led Britain and France to form an alliance that pledged to resist further German attacks. In June 1939, Hitler signed a treaty with the Soviet Union. The pact allowed the Soviet government a free hand to annex several European regions, including Bessarabia.

World War II

After Germany attacked Poland in the fall of 1939, World War II broke out in Europe. Romania declared its neutrality at the start of the war. In 1940 the Soviet Union demanded that Romania give up Bessarabia. Soviet troops then invaded

Courtesy of National Archives

Romanian cavalry cross the Prut River into Bessarabia in 1941, as Romania joins the German attack on the Soviet Union. By the end of World War II (1939–1945), the Soviet army occupied Bessarabia as well as Romania.

the region, renaming it the Moldavian Soviet Socialist Republic. Romania, with a far weaker army, could do nothing to prevent the Soviet takeover.

As German armies continued to gain victories throughout 1940, Carol agreed under pressure from Hitler to give up Romanian land to Bulgaria, to the Soviet Union, and to Hungary. Hitler also demanded access to Romania's valuable oil supplies. In September 1940, General Ion Antonescu, a Romanian military leader allied with the Iron Guard, took control of the government and forced Carol to resign. Carol's son Michael became the legal ruler of the country, although Antonescu controlled the army and the government.

Antonescu allowed German forces to enter the country and, in June 1941, ordered the Romanian army to join the Germans in a surprise attack on the Soviet Union. Romanian forces poured into Soviet Moldavia and across southern Ukraine. But in 1943 a terrible defeat at Stalingrad in central Russia stopped the Romanian advance. By 1944 the tide had turned, and Soviet forces were throwing back the Germans and Romanians.

Antonescu came under attack from the monarch and from his political rivals, who opposed the alliance with Hitler. In August 1944, King Michael joined with several political groups to overthrow Antonescu. Romania then signed a peace treaty with the Soviet Union. A new government—made up of Romania's prewar parties as well as the Romanian Communist party—took power.

As the German armies retreated in the spring of 1945, Soviet forces drove through eastern Europe. Many of the region's weak and unstable governments came under pressure from the Soviet Union, which sought to extend its political and economic control into the Balkan Peninsula. Although Romania regained territory taken by Bulgaria and Hungary in 1940, the Soviet Union reoccupied Soviet Moldavia.

Photo by Paul E. Michelson

A stamp celebrating the Communist takeover of Romania bears the former Romanian flag and symbols of the country's industrialization.

Postwar Development

In 1947 Romania's Communist leaders forced King Michael to resign. With the support of the Soviet army, which was occupying Romania, the Communists drove all competing parties out of the government and had many opposition leaders arrested. Politicians, writers, and university professors were executed or jailed in concentration camps for criticizing the regime. The government also began to nationalize (take over) banks, industries, and mines.

In the next year, Romania adopted a new constitution that put the country under the leadership of a five-member state council. In 1952 Gheorghe Gheorgiu-Dej, the first secretary (leader) of the Romanian Communist party, became the prime minister.

Under Soviet direction, new industrial companies were formed to control production of steel, oil, coal, and other important goods. These companies sent much of their output and half of their profits back to the

President Nicolae Ceausescu speaks at a celebration of his sixtieth birthday in 1978. Although Ceausescu ruled Romania as the head of a state council, he held absolute power over the country's foreign and domestic policies.

Soviet Union. Romania's private farmers were forced to combine their holdings into collective farms, where crop production was under government direction.

Romania enjoyed impressive economic growth in the 1950s and 1960s. The government developed new industries, built schools, and installed electric power in many remote villages. But Soviet control of the economy prompted many Romanians to call for greater independence. In the mid-1960s, Romania forged closer trade ties with non-Communist nations in western Europe.

In 1965 Nicolae Ceausescu became the head of the Communist party in Romania. He and two other Communist leaders ruled in a coalition until 1967, when Ceausescu became the president of the state council. At a party congress (meeting) in 1974, Ceausescu was elected Romania's president.

In the late 1960s, Ceausescu claimed increasing independence for Romania and called on Soviet leaders to withdraw their forces from eastern Europe. In the 1970s, Ceausescu made several trips to the United States, with which he signed an economic pact. Romania also made agreements with the European Community, a trade alliance of western European nations.

Recent Events

Within Romania, however, Ceausescu enforced a strict regime. Government bureaus censored all Romanian media, and the government continued to jail its opponents. Although economic growth continued in the 1970s, prices rose as well, and Romanians began to suffer shortages of food and consumer goods.

The Communist system of central planning and state ownership of the economy resulted in corruption and inefficiency. Many industries used outdated equipment, and the government did not invest in new machinery. In addition, Ceausescu used public funds for massive building projects in Bucharest and for lavish personal expenses.

To pay for its industrial growth, Romania borrowed heavily from western nations. Determined to repay this debt, Ceausescu saved money by limiting imports of essential food, energy, and consumer goods. These policies and the falling production in Romanian factories further damaged the economy in the late 1980s.

Discontent with Communist rule erupted into violence in the late 1980s. In December 1989, a demonstration against Ceausescu in Timisoara ended in a massacre by security forces. Street battles in Bucharest and Brasov killed hundreds of people. As riots continued in the capital, several army units joined the anti-Communist demonstrators. When Ceausescu attempted to flee, he was captured and quickly executed.

Ceausescu's fall brought to power the National Salvation Front, a party led by former Communist officials. Ion Iliescu, the organization's leader, became the Romanian president. Open elections in 1990 gave the Front a majority in the legislature. In 1992 Iliescu defeated his opponents again in a presidential election. Although many politicians are critical of Iliescu, they have been unable to unite behind a single leader and challenge the National Salvation Front.

Many Romanians believe that the country's leaders, as former members of the Communist party, have little interest in returning Romania to a democratic system of government. Protests against the

Photo by Patricia Drentea/Visuals Unlimited

Citizens of Bucharest examine announcements posted in University Square. Romania's Communist regime tightly controlled newspapers, television, and radio broadcasts. As a result, during the 1989 revolution, many Romanians got much of their information from wall posters.

National Salvation Front have led to violence in Bucharest. In addition, foreign countries are reluctant to make new investments while Romania's political situation remains unstable.

Government

Voters approved Romania's new constitution on December 8, 1991. The legislature, known as the Grand National Assembly, is made up of two chambers—the 397-member Chamber of Deputies and the 119-member Senate. Voters aged 18 and older elect members to four-year terms.

The official head of government is a president, who is elected by a popular vote to a term of four years. The president, who is also the commander in chief of the Romanian armed forces, may serve a maximum of two terms. The president names the prime minister, who selects a cabinet of 23 members. Cabinet members and the prime minister must be confirmed by the legislature.

The Supreme Court is Romania's highest court of appeals. Each county has its own court, and there are also lower courts that hear criminal and civil cases.

Romania is divided into 40 counties and the municipal district of Bucharest. The country's urban areas include 260 towns and 2,699 communes. Local councils administer Romanian cities and towns.

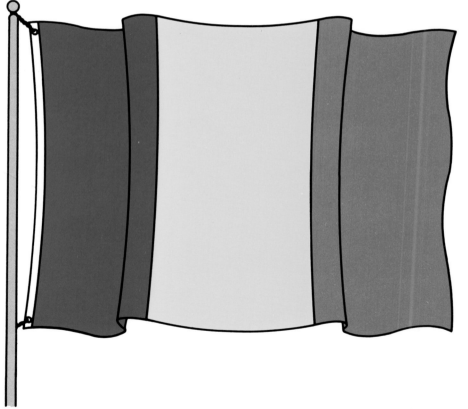

Artwork by Laura Westlund

Until 1989 Romania's flag carried the official state emblem, which included the symbolic red star of the Communist party. Romania's government has since removed the seal. The flag's colors represent Transylvania, Moldavia, and Wallachia— Romania's three largest regions.

Photo by Patricia Drentea/Visuals Unlimited

Members of a Romanian family attend a ceremony at a gravesite, where they leave cakes, candles, and flowers to celebrate the memory of a loved one.

3) The People

Although Romania was once an agricultural country, the Communist leaders who came to power after World War II encouraged the growth of industry. In the 1960s and 1970s, factory jobs brought many people into the cities from the countryside. As a result, Romania's large cities—especially Bucharest—have grown rapidly during the last 40 years. Slightly more than half of Romania's 23.2 million people live in cities and towns.

At the same time, the population in many rural areas of Romania declined. The establishment of state-owned farming collectives under Communist rule forced many farmers off their land. In 1988 the government began destroying Romanian villages and moving their inhabitants into newly built high-rise apartment buildings. Rural people strongly resisted this policy, however, and with the fall of Ceausescu the program came to a halt.

Most Romanians inhabit Wallachia and Moldavia, regions with productive plains and fertile river valleys. About one-third of the nation's people live in the foothills of the Carpathian Mountains and in the uplands of Transylvania. Mountainous areas and the unproductive lowlands of Dobrogea have the country's lowest population density.

Ethnic Groups

Throughout its history, Romania has been home to a wide variety of ethnic groups. The original Dacian inhabitants intermarried with Romans and with peoples that moved into the Balkan Peninsula from northern Europe. Hungarians and Germans later settled in Transylvania and Banat. The Black Sea coast and the Dobrogea region, which contain important transportation routes, attracted settlers from many parts of eastern Europe as well as Turkey. Modern Romania includes more than 20 ethnic minorities.

Ethnic Romanians, who make up 88 percent of the population, have dominated the political and cultural life of the country since its final unification in the early twentieth century. Moldavia and Wallachia, the first independent Romanian states, have the highest concentration of Romanians. Small numbers of Romanian-speakers also live in the Balkan nations of Greece, Bulgaria, and Croatia. Northeast of Romania is the newly independent nation of Moldova, formerly Soviet Moldavia. This territory still has an ethnic Romanian majority and close cultural ties to Romania.

About 8 percent of Romanian citizens claim Hungarian ancestry. Most of the country's Hungarians live in Banat and Transylvania. Hungarians make up a majority in the region surrounding the city of Tirgu-Mures, near the geographic center of Romania. For several centuries, Transylvania was under Hungarian control, and political conflict has occurred between Romanians and Hungarians who live in the region.

Also inhabiting Transylvania are ethnic Germans, who settled in the region at the invitation of Hungarian kings in the twelfth and thirteenth centuries. Descen-

Photo by Bernice Condit

Women offer goods for sale at a bus stop in rural Romania. Some rural villages lack stores, so townspeople do their shopping at small, open-air markets.

A farmer drives his cart through a Hungarian village in Covasna, a region in the Carpathian Mountains with a large ethnic Hungarian population.

dants of German farmers who arrived in the eighteenth century still live in Banat.

Jews in Romania number about 20,000. Throughout Romania's history, Jews settled in northern Moldavia and in Bucharest. Many earned a living as merchants and traders in Romanian cities. During World War II, Jews suffered persecution by both the Romanian government and the German army. After the war, many Jews emigrated to Israel, a Middle Eastern state.

In Dobrogea less than half the population is Romanian. Ethnic Tatars, as well as descendants of the Ottoman Turks, inhabit the region. Romania has one of

Europe's largest populations of Gypsies, a nomadic people who live in small rural settlements and on the outskirts of many Romanian cities and towns.

Religion

Romania's Communist leaders passed many laws to restrict religious worship. The government closed or destroyed churches, seized church lands, and arrested members of the clergy. Government-controlled media sharply criticized religious faith and practices.

Despite these restrictions, no religions were subject to outright bans, and many

43

This church occupies the Curtea de Arges (Court of Arges), a monastery in the foothills of the Carpathian Mountains. The designers of the fourteenth-century church adopted the popular architectural style of the Byzantine Empire.

Uniate Church, this faith has survived with more than one million members, most of whom are ethnic Romanians.

Romania's Jewish population has steadily declined since World War II. Nevertheless, Judaism has remained an active faith among Jewish communities that have survived in Bucharest and in Moldavia. Most of the Tatars and Turks living in the Dobrogea region are Muslims—followers of the Islamic religion.

Art and Music

Romanian painting dates back to ancient times, when Dacian potters decorated their wares with elaborate geometric designs. The painting and architecture of the Byzantine Empire influenced artists and builders in the emerging principalities of Wallachia and Moldavia. The monastery of Curtea de Arges, in Wallachia, strongly reflects Byzantine styles. At the Moldavian monastery of Voronet, founded during the reign of Stephen the Great, frescoes (paintings done on wet plaster) decorate interior and exterior walls. The artists of Voronet depicted biblical scenes, as well as the struggles of the Romanian people against the Ottoman Turks.

Painting in Romania reached an artistic peak during the 1800s, when many Romanian artists studied at academies in western Europe. The painter Theodor Aman, a famous portraitist, worked in a traditional style. Nicolae Grigorescu illustrated rural people in the natural settings of his landscape paintings.

After World War II, socialist realism became the dominant style of Romanian art. Socialist realism required artists to render industrial workers and Communist leaders in flattering or heroic poses. The government forced all of the country's artists to join a tightly controlled union and forbade the use of abstract shapes and symbols in painting and sculpture.

Nevertheless, the most famous Romanian artist of the postwar period was Con-

Romanians kept their beliefs. The Romanian Orthodox Church remained the largest religious institution in Romania. More than 70 percent of the population belongs to this church, which is a branch of the Eastern Orthodox Church.

Many Hungarians and Germans living in Romania belong to the Roman Catholic Church. Most non-Catholic Germans living in Transylvania are Lutherans, a Protestant denomination that split from the Catholic church in the sixteenth century. An important branch of Catholicism in Romania is the Uniate Church, whose members accept the authority of the Catholic pope but practice Orthodox religious rites. Although the Communist government took harsh measures against the

Folk dancers perform in a crowded Romanian restaurant. Traditional dancing is still popular among Romanian city dwellers, many of whom arrived from rural areas after World War II.

stantin Brancusi, an abstract sculptor who lived in France. Brancusi molded wood and bright metal into long shapes and geometric forms to idealize people and nature. Museums and private collectors around the world have purchased Brancusi's elegant sculptures.

Romania also has a strong tradition of folk art and handicrafts. Weavers still produce rugs by knotting natural wool yarn on wooden looms. Furniture from different regions of the country carries elaborate designs in a variety of materials. Traditional linen and clothing are still common in many rural homes in Romania.

Music is a favorite pastime in Romania, where symphony orchestras, soloists, and choirs perform. Residents and visitors enjoy folk and jazz festivals held in Bucharest. Many professional and amateur groups perform the national dance, the *hora*, and folk songs known as *dainas*.

Romania's best-known classical musician is Georges Enesco, a violinist who wrote

Constantin Brancusi worked in both wood and metal to create elegant abstract sculptures, such as this *Portrait of Nancy Cunard*.

45

a famous series of rhapsodies based on Romanian folk melodies. Bucharest holds a festival of Enesco's music every three years. The Romanian pianist Dinu Lipatti gained international recognition as a performer and orchestral conductor.

Language and Literature

Like French and other Romance languages, Romanian is based on ancient Latin. In the centuries since the Roman occupation of historic Dacia, Greek, Slavic, and Turkish words have been introduced into the Romanian vocabulary. In the fourteenth century, Romanians adopted the Cyrillic alphabet, which is also used in the Slavic languages of Russian and Ukrainian. To emphasize their Roman origins, Romanians in Transylvania later returned to the Latin alphabet. The entire nation eventually adopted Latin lettering.

The German and Hungarian communities in Transylvania and Banat are bilingual, meaning they use their own languages as well as Romanian. Both Hungarian and Romanian are common in Cluj, a bilingual Transylvanian city. Although the Ceausescu government banned non-Romanian media, Hungarian and German newspapers and television programs reappeared in the early 1990s.

The earliest Romanian literary works were ballads—poetry that was set to music and sung aloud from memory. Orthodox church leaders wrote the first Romanian religious texts in the fifteenth century. Romanian historians of the 1700s, including Dimitri Cantemir, proudly traced the story of their nation back to the settlement of the country by the Romans.

In the 1800s, a group of authors helped pave the way for the unification of Romania. They drew on Romanian folklore to inspire their audiences. The Romanian legend of Dracula, which combined history and myth, became famous through the works of foreign authors. After the country won its independence in the late nineteenth century, many Romanian authors wrote plays and poetry. Mihai Eminescu, a poet from Moldavia, penned lyric and epic verse about Romanian history and culture. Ion Luca Caragiale, one of the most popular authors of the time, wrote comic plays about Romanian politics.

Romanians have contributed to modern styles in both art and literature. The writer Tristan Tzara, who left Romania during World War I, settled in France and took part in the dadaist movement, which attacked conventional art forms. Eugene Ionesco also spent much of his life in France, where he became a famous playwright. His works, including *The Bald Soprano* and *Rhinoceros,* amuse audiences with their descriptions of the absurdities of modern life.

Health and Education

Under the Communist government, spending on public health increased, and most health care in Romania was provided free

Photo by Paul E. Michelson

A bust of the nineteenth-century Romanian national poet Mihai Eminescu stands in a Bucharest park.

Photo by Caroline Penn

Many ethnic Germans are leaving Romania, and only 4 pupils remain in this German school in a Transylvanian village. The German government donates books and materials to the school, which once had as many as sixty students.

of charge. After World War II, the number of physicians and hospital beds rose sharply. But much of the improvement has taken place in Romania's cities, leaving rural areas and villages with poor facilities and a shortage of trained doctors.

Romania encouraged population growth through strict laws against birth control and through financial support of families with children. Poor economic conditions, however, discourage many Romanians from having large families. With 12 babies born for every 1,000 people, Romania's birthrate is lower than average in eastern Europe. At its present growth rate of 0.1 percent, Romania's population will not double for 578 years.

The infant mortality rate in Romania— about 26 deaths per 1,000 live births—is one of the highest rates in Europe. Many infant deaths are caused by food shortages, poor care for expectant mothers, or inadequate medical facilities. Abandoned infants crowd state institutions, where the rate of hepatitis and AIDS is high. Romania's average life expectancy is 70

years, a low figure among eastern European countries. Cancer, heart disease, and alcoholism are the most serious health problems among adults. Environmental pollution also affects public health in many Romanian cities.

The government requires children between the ages of 6 and 16 to attend school. Elementary school lasts for eight years. Students must then take examinations to pass to secondary schools, which take two years to complete. About half of all Romanian secondary students enroll in vocational schools, where they learn basic job skills. Others attend technical institutes or teacher-training colleges.

About 5 percent of Romania's secondary students take courses that prepare them for universities. The country's largest, the University of Bucharest, was established in 1864. Students must pass difficult examinations to enter postsecondary schools. Because few families can afford the tutoring necessary to pass these tests, children of farmers or factory laborers rarely achieve a university education.

47

In a private home, an Orthodox priest presides at a dinner held in the memory of a relative.

Photo by Patricia Drentea/Visuals Unlimited

A Romanian family gathers in the afternoon for tea and sweet pastries.

Photo by Patricia Drentea/Visuals Unlimited

Food

Romanian cuisine has a rich tradition that borrows from Turkish and Greek cooking. A favorable climate and fertile soil contribute to the wide variety of vegetables and grains used in Romanian dishes. One of the most popular recipes is *mititei*—grilled beef eaten as an appetizer or as a main course. *Branzeturi* (cheeses) are also served before or during meals.

A light Romanian breakfast may include rolls, butter and jam, as well as tea or milk. Romanians enjoy their principal meal in the early afternoon. For a first course,

cooks prepare soups with meat, vegetables, or noodles. *Borsh* is a thick cabbage soup traditionally made with bran. *Ciorba* are soups cooked with lamb, mushrooms, leeks, or other meats and vegetables.

Popular main courses are *tocana*, a pork stew served with garlic and onions, and *mamaliga*, a dish of cornmeal. Stuffed cabbage, vine leaves, or poached eggs are often eaten with mamaliga. Rice and minced meat are wrapped in vine or cabbage leaves to make *sarmale*. Vegetables such as eggplant, peppers, or gherkins often accompany the main course.

48

Romanian desserts include ice cream, cakes, pastries, pies known as *placinte*, and *baclava*—a thin pastry filled with nuts and covered with honey syrup. *Papanasi* are doughnuts made with cream and cheese. Adults also enjoy a wide variety of excellent wines, most of which are produced in Moldavia and along the Black Sea coast.

Recreation and Sports

The Carpathian Mountains and the Black Sea coast are the busiest recreation spots in Romania. Rock climbing, hiking, and snow skiing are popular in the Carpathians. Vacation resorts along the Black Sea offer swimming, sailing, waterskiing, and other warm-weather sports.

The country's favorite spectator sport is soccer. The government has built soccer stadiums in Romania's large cities and has organized soccer leagues. Many amateur sports clubs participate in cycling, soccer, and tennis. An 80,000-seat stadium in Bucharest hosts basketball, volleyball, handball, and skating.

Independent Picture Service

Visitors to this modern resort in the Carpathians enjoy skiing in the deep mountain snow.

Romanian Olympic athletes have brought home medals in gymnastics, wrestling, and weightlifting. The famous Romanian gymnast Nadia Comaneci was the first athlete in history to earn perfect scores of 10 for gymnastic routines she performed during the 1976 summer Olympic Games in Montreal, Canada.

Independent Picture Service

The beaches on the Black Sea near Constanta are a popular spot for swimming, sailing, and lying in the sun. Romanians, as well as tourists from other parts of Europe, relax at the Black Sea coast every summer.

Shoppers wait for a food store in Bucharest to open. Many goods in Romania continue to be in short supply.

4) The Economy

Romania's economy went through a transformation in the years after World War II. The postwar Communist government nationalized industries, mines, banks, transportation companies, and most retail stores. Government planners managed these new state-owned businesses, drawing up production schedules based on a series of five-year plans. Soviet leaders formed Soviet-Romanian companies that were run for the benefit of the Soviet Union. Although these joint ventures ended in 1954, the Soviet Union remained Romania's most important trading partner.

Lacking money for investment, Romania went heavily into debt to pay for new construction. In the 1960s and 1970s, to pay back this debt, the Romanian government exported most of the country's manufactured products and imported very little. This policy resulted in severe shortages of consumer goods and even of food.

After the fall of the Communist government in 1989, Romania's new leaders tried to create a more open market for goods and services. The government also offered state-owned businesses for sale to private investors. But competition among Romanian companies—many of which use outdated equipment and production methods —is causing some enterprises to fail. In addition, since wages are still low and the government no longer controls prices, many Romanians cannot afford to buy consumer goods.

The country's industrialization has also caused severe damage to Romania's natural environment. The government has done little to regulate pollution, and factories and mines have fouled the air and water. The country's poor economic conditions are making environmental cleanup expensive and difficult. Many Romanians suffer serious health problems as a result.

Industry

Romania began a program of intensive industrial development in the 1950s and 1960s. Government-owned firms built new plants throughout the country, and the cities of Bucharest, Cluj, Brasov, and Timisoara became important manufacturing centers. The Communist leadership invested in heavy industries that made durable goods, such as machinery and steel. These businesses still dominate Romania's manufacturing sector, which employed nearly 40 percent of the labor force in the early 1990s.

The assembly of machines and vehicles has long been the largest manufacturing business in Romania. Because the government severely restricted imports, farm and industrial equipment had to be built inside the country. Romanian plants also have produced airplanes, oil-drilling rigs, ships, and railroad cars.

Factories in Bucharest and Galati, a city on the lower Danube, make cement and steel for the construction industry. The manufacture of aluminum, copper, and other finished metals is also important in

Photo by Caroline Penn

This Transylvanian factory produces lampblack, a pigment used in making paints and inks. Pollution from the factory coats nearby streets and homes with dust and soot.

Workers assemble engine parts in a car factory. After World War II, the Romanian government built new factories in order to lessen the country's dependence on imported goods, such as cars, ships, and heavy machinery.

construction and for export. Refineries convert crude oil and other petroleum products into rubber and chemicals. Other plants make electrical equipment, such as radios and televisions, as well as textiles, shoes, and finished clothing.

Many of the country's industries are suffering financial problems. The state has sold some businesses to private investors and has allowed joint ventures with foreign companies. The outdated equipment used in many plants hurts the quality of Romanian products, and businesses are finding it difficult to compete with other European firms on the world market.

Agriculture

Between 1948 and 1962, the Romanian government took over most of the country's private farms, forcing rural workers to join state-owned collective farms. Each collective had a planning committee, which set schedules and production goals. Farmers shared their labor and income. By the 1960s, the Romanian government owned 90 percent of the country's productive land.

Collectivization, however, did not improve harvests in Romania. Because the government invested mostly in heavy industries, little money was available for

Romanian farmers once used windmills to grind harvested grain. This windmill was moved from the Danube delta to the Village Museum in Bucharest.

Photo by Caroline Penn

Farmers in Covasna stack beets, which will later be refined into sugar. A lack of machinery forces many farmers to harvest their crops by hand.

farm improvements. In addition, the government moved workers from the countryside to the cities, leaving rural areas with a shortage of farm laborers.

In the early 1990s, the government began returning farmland to private ownership. Farmers have taken advantage of a free market for their goods, and the production of meat and grain has slowly increased. Outdated farming methods and equipment, however, continue to limit crop yields.

Romania's principal crops are grains—including wheat, rye, and corn—that grow on the plains of Wallachia, Moldavia, and Banat. Farmers raise sunflowers for their seeds and oil and grow beets to be refined into sugar. Wine grapes thrive in Moldavia and near the Black Sea coast. Mountainous regions of Romania support fruit orchards and grape vineyards. Livestock raised in Romania include cattle, pigs, sheep, goats, horses, and poultry.

Photo by Patricia Drentea/Visuals Unlimited

A storage bin in Moldavia holds ears of corn, which will feed livestock during the winter months.

53

Travelers wait for their train to arrive at a Bucharest station. Several Romanian rail lines end at Bucharest, which also has connections to other nations in eastern Europe.

Energy and Transportation

The oil fields in Romania's southern and eastern Carpathian Mountains have provided an important source of energy since the late nineteenth century. But the country's oil reserves are falling rapidly, and new drilling projects have been only partially successful. Oil now meets only a small percentage of the country's heating and electricity needs. Substantial deposits of coal and natural gas fuel most of Romania's power plants, although reserves of these resources are also declining.

Hydroelectric stations on the Danube and its tributaries provided about 17 percent of Romania's electricity in the early 1990s. Romania also generates power from wind, solar energy, methane gas, and heated underground water.

Romania's railroad network connects major cities and ports and includes about 7,000 miles of track. Railroad projects

A road marker lists destinations and distances along a Romanian highway.

Trolley cars roll through downtown Bucharest. Many city dwellers lack automobiles and instead use buses, trolleys, and bicycles to travel around the capital.

A shepherd directs his flock across a rural highway in Wallachia's Olt River Valley. Romania's transportation network includes 40,000 miles of roads.

55

completed in the 1980s increased the rail system's capacity, but only about 10 percent of the nation's freight moves by train. Romanian State Railways provides passenger rail service. In addition, an underground rail system transports people in Bucharest.

Romania's road network consists of 40,000 miles of paved and unpaved routes. Most roads have two lanes, but construction of a network of modern, four-lane highways is under way. Tarom (Romanian Air Lines), the state-owned airline, serves regional centers and coastal resorts. International airports have been built near Bucharest and Constanta.

River traffic has long been important to Romania's foreign trade. Commercial barges use the Danube River, the busiest waterway of central and eastern Europe. A canal connects the river with Constanta, Romania's principal port on the Black Sea. Passenger ferries also link Black Sea ports with cities along the Danube River.

Buckets of coal are transported from a mine to a processing plant. Coal-burning power stations supply most of Romania's energy.

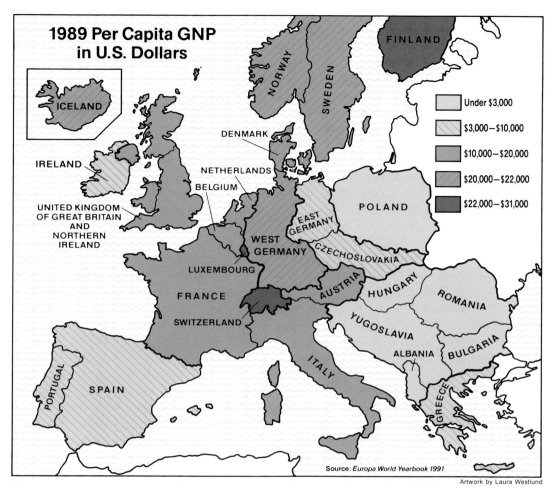

1989 Per Capita GNP in U.S. Dollars

Under $3,000

$3,000 – $10,000

$10,000 – $20,000

$20,000 – $22,000

$22,000 – $31,000

Source: *Europa World Yearbook 1991*

Artwork by Laura Westlund

This map compares the average wealth per person – calculated by gross national product (GNP) per capita – for 26 European countries in 1989. The GNP is the value of all goods and services produced by a country in a year. To arrive at the GNP per capita, each nation's total GNP is divided by its population. The resulting amounts indicate one measure of the standard of living in each country. Romania's figure of $2,560 – one of the lowest in Europe – reflects the country's declining manufacturing sector, which has been hurt by outdated machinery and production methods.

Foreign Trade

For many years, Romania's most important trading partner was the Soviet Union, which closely linked its economy with those of eastern European countries. Soviet raw materials arrived in Romanian factories, which shipped finished goods back to the Soviet Union. But Romania also formed trading ties with many non-Communist countries, particularly Germany. The former Soviet republics and Germany are still Romania's biggest trad-

ing partners. Romania also trades with Italy, China, Iran, and eastern Europe.

Fuels and raw materials make up the largest portion of Romania's foreign trade. Machinery, chemicals, furniture, textiles, aluminum, and steel products are important exports. To meet its energy needs, Romania imports coal, natural gas, and crude oil. Romanian companies also buy sugar, meat, iron ore, and cotton from abroad.

Severe restrictions on imports in the 1970s and 1980s contributed to a trade

Castle Peles *(above),* **a royal estate built by King Carol II, has become a popular tourist attraction. The castle lies on a hill** *(below)* **that rises above Sinaia, a small village in the Carpathian Mountains.**

surplus, meaning that Romania earned more from exports than it spent on imports. As a result, Romania has some money available for acquiring new products from other countries. The favorable balance of trade may also make it easier for the government to plan for future economic growth.

Tourism

In the early 1990s, Romania attracted several million tourists each year, and tourist spending totaled more than $200 million annually. Since the fall of Communist governments in eastern Europe, tourism has become an important source of income. Newly opened borders allow an increasing number of western European tourists to visit the region.

Artists and tourists enjoy the colorful frescoes (paintings made on wet plaster) that decorate many Moldavian churches.

Romania offers a variety of attractions and activities. Rural villages in Transylvania and in the northern Carpathians provide glimpses into a traditional way of life that is nearly extinct in Europe. Romania's magnificent castles, including the imposing Bran Castle near Brasov, display distinctive exterior and interior design. The monasteries of Moldavia draw religious pilgrims and art lovers who admire the centuries-old frescoes that adorn the monasteries' walls.

As late as the nineteenth century, some rural Romanian families built their homes underground for protection from Turkish attacks.

Photo by Caroline Penn

A child stands near an elaborately carved wooden doorway. Wood carving remains a popular craft throughout Romania.

The old neighborhoods of Brasov, Sibiu, and Cluj have survived Romania's industrialization and modernization. Bucharest offers visitors fine museums and music festivals. The Village Museum in the capital preserves examples of traditional homes from around the country. Tourists who favor recreational activities visit the Carpathian Mountains for hiking and the Black Sea coast for sailing, swimming, and waterskiing.

The Future

Romanians face a difficult transition from dictatorship to democracy. Under the rule of Nicolae Ceausescu, non-Communist political parties could not operate openly, and opponents of the regime risked arrest for expressing their views. Ceausescu's sudden and violent overthrow left some

Photo by Patricia Drentea/Visuals Unlimited

Modern apartments rise in Focsani, a city in Moldavia. After World War II, the Romanian government replaced old neighborhoods in Focsani and other cities with high-rise housing for industrial workers.

A father strolls with his child through a park in the Transylvanian city of Tirgu-Mures.

A German woman lives by herself in a small Transylvanian village. When Romania opened its borders after the fall of Ceausescu's regime, the woman's children and grandchildren took the opportunity to emigrate to Germany.

Newspapers and magazines attract browsers along a sidewalk in Bucharest. The government has lifted most controls on Romania's printed media.

The national theater in the capital stages the works of Romania's famous playwrights.

A Gypsy holds her child in Bucharest. A nomadic people who live in small villages and in poor urban neighborhoods, Gypsies suffer a very high rate of unemployment. Many of them have left Romania to escape poverty and malnutrition.

Photo © Connie Bickman/GEO Imagery

Romanians unprepared for a representative government.

Lacking strong and independent political parties, the new Romanian parliament is having difficulty in putting new economic policies in place. Without improvement in the economy, Romanian consumers will continue to suffer from low wages, shortages of consumer goods, and a poor standard of living.

Despite the promise of open elections, strong opposition to the National Salvation Front—Romania's majority political party—has continued. Violence between antigovernment demonstrators and police has occurred in Bucharest. Many feel that protests prompted by the worsening economy could result in a direct attack on the government. To prevent this, Romania's leaders must tackle economic problems while maintaining the country's newly won political freedoms.

Photo by Patricia Drentea/Visuals Unlimited

In Bucharest, cranes and scaffolds surround buildings heavily damaged by the violent rebellion of December 1989.

Index